GOD
WITH
US

25 Advent Reflections
J.John

Published in the UK by Philo Trust

Copyright © 2014 J.John

Published 2014 by Philo Trust, Witton House, Lower Road, Chorleywood,
Rickmansworth, WD3 5LB, United Kingdom

www.philotrust.com

The right of J.John to be identified as the Author of this Work has been asserted by
him in accordance with the Copyright, Designs and Patents Act 1988.

British Library Cataloguing in Publication Data

A catalogue record for this book is available from the British Library

ISBN: 978-0-9928399-4-9

Design by Rachel Fung

Typeset by Verité CM Ltd

Printed and bound in the UK

CONTENTS

PREFACE

The Early Church took very seriously the startling idea that, in the birth of Jesus, God himself had come to Earth in person. In fact, they took it so seriously that they calculated the date of the Nativity (wrongly, as it turned out) and used it to divide all history into BC and AD. And precisely because the feast that became Christmas celebrated an event that was so utterly earth-shattering, they believed that it was inappropriate that it should occur without some preparations. They did not, it seems, feel that it was right that anyone should routinely walk into church only to suddenly realise that the focus of the day's worship was about the biggest event of history. A commemoration of something as big as Christmas – the infinite God becoming a few pounds of human flesh – could not be allowed to just happen; people needed to be prepared for it. So it became the habit to have a season of preparation before Christmas Day. That period soon acquired the title 'Advent' from the Latin word *adventus* or 'coming', a word that highlighted how this season focused on the coming of Jesus as a baby in Bethlehem. And, in various forms, Advent has been with us ever since.

Let me explain a little what I see Advent as being all about. To return to that word *adventus*: 'coming'. To summarise, in Advent Christians celebrate Christ's coming in three ways. First, we celebrate his coming in history; secondly, we look to his coming again in the future; and thirdly, we look to his coming into our lives. Let me unpack each of these a little.

Advent looks back in time. It points to the moment in history when God intervened in a way that was completely beyond expectation and utterly beyond imagination. Somehow, in Mary's womb, God became one of us; united completely and permanently with humanity. At the first Christmas, God came on our side and the great rescue of the human race began. This is a tremendous encouragement: Christmas reminds us that God is committed to the world and to its rescue.

Yet if the message of Advent looks back to the past, it also looks forward to the future. There is a promise in this season that the work that was begun at the first Christmas will, one day – at a time and in a manner beyond guessing – be gloriously completed. The first coming of Christ was in obscurity and humility; his second coming will be unmistakable and glorious. We can look forward in hope. One day there will be a new and infinitely greater Christmas Day; Jesus will return, not as a baby, but as King.

The third element of the Advent season is the idea that runs through these meditations. Christ did not simply come as Saviour and Redeemer of the physical universe or of humankind in general; he came as the Saviour of individuals, people like you and me. We may believe wonderful things about the coming of Christ to the world, but the fact remains that these truths are totally meaningless unless we have taken them and applied them for ourselves. The message of Advent is that Christ came for individual *people*: not just Mary, Joseph and those other characters who are in the Bible story, but for you and for me. Advent is not just about an event in history – however significant – it is about an offer that you and I must accept.

This then is, in summary, what Advent stands for. Now let me suggest three good reasons why and how we should pay attention to Advent.

First, Advent should be a time of **anticipation**. Traditionally the season of Advent was one of messages, meditations and prayers that gradually lead us towards the coming of Christ into the world at Christmas time. It was the great warm-up for the greatest of all events and I think creating this season of preparation was a wise idea because it helped make Christmas truly sacred. The problem today is that we don't like waiting: we want it *now*. Ours is the age of instant everything: microwave suppers, credit on demand and even speed-dating. The trouble is that speed costs and one price we must pay is the loss of the experience of anticipation. Anticipation is the worthwhile side of waiting and it is a good thing; there is something especially thrilling about looking forward to what you don't have but will get one day. One of the certain markers that the 'festive season' is upon us is going into the supermarket and hearing the weary old pop song 'I Wish It Could Be Christmas Every Day'. Whatever you think about it as music, the sentiment is dreadful. If Christmas was every day, it would be worthless. We all know that part of the fun of presents is undoing the wrapping and Advent acts as the wrapping paper around Christmas. Waiting is worthwhile.

Now you might argue that with the Christmas season starting (at least for retailers) in late September there is enough waiting for Christmas already. Actually, the sheer busyness of this time of the year (the shopping, the cards, the cooking) means that even Christians can find that the true celebration of what Christmas is about gets left until the very last moment. We need to remind ourselves that the best things in life are those that should not be hastened. Whether the good thing is a meal, a conversation, or even a marriage, there are the appropriate and necessary preliminaries that should not be omitted: haste is waste. Advent is the slow, careful preparation for the great event of Christmas and we neglect it to our loss.

One thing I am hoping with this series of daily reflections is that they will encourage a sense of anticipation.

Second, Advent should be a time of **attention**. One of the problems with celebrating Advent today is that it is, in every sense, the noisiest part of the year. We have let commerce and business hijack this season so that what was once spiritual has now become utterly material: an exhausting and seemingly unending crescendo of consumerism. The glare of the Christmas lights blinds us to Advent's lessons, and the noise of commercials makes God's message too easily inaudible. Jesus has become buried under toys and tinsel, the Christ-child suffocated by synthetic snow.

The noise that the world generates at this time is so overwhelming that it is all too easy to reduce our Christianity to the most basic truths: sometimes little more than 'a special baby was born'. The awesome reality is that the coming of God to Earth in Jesus has infinite importance and we would be wise to pay it the closest attention. Christmas says – amongst many things – that God cares for the world, that he has become one with the human race, that he intends to redeem us, that he has come out of heaven in person to battle evil. In the deepest and most hopeless darkness, Christmas shouts out that God has brought light and hope into the world. There is a depth to Christmas that it is easy to lose. Part of my motive in writing these reflections is to help us pay attention, day by day, to more of what this tremendous season of the year should mean for us.

Thirdly, Advent should be a time of **application**. If you ask people what they expect from Christmas you get the idea that they want good feelings. They want to have a happy experience, they want to enjoy themselves and they want to have their spirits lifted. That is great as far as it goes, but it is very superficial. Emotions never changed the world. The reality is that Advent and the Christmas celebrations that it leads up to should not simply be a time of fun but rather a period where we apply God's truth to our lives – be humbled as you see Almighty God descend to become a baby. If you watch the news and feel that the world is beyond hope, turn to Christmas and be cheered because Jesus' birth tells us that God is committed to sorting out the mess of this world. If your difficulties and problems threaten to overwhelm you, turn to Christmas and be encouraged as you realise that because of it God is prepared to stand alongside you through the very worst that life can throw at you.

I believe that an understanding of Advent and Christmas can transform our lives and because of that I have tried in these reflections to focus on people more than principles. This is the most practical of seasons.

Advent looks forward to the world in every way being utterly changed by the coming of Christ. As you follow these reflections on Advent may your life be transformed in a similar way through God: Father, Son and Holy Spirit.

J.John

1st December

INTRODUCTION

If you read the Bible for the first time, your first impression might well be that it is full of people with unusual names: *Happuch, Makbannai, Ozem, Shabbethai* and *Tryphosa*! Of course, the exotic names are just a fact of history: most of the events of the Bible happened a long time ago in what we now call the Middle East.

The Bible is a story involving people. We live in a world where people are becoming less important. We are no longer Mr and Mrs X but 'consumers', 'subscribers', 'voters' or 'occupiers' at an address. Even worse, to many organisations and institutions, we seem to be no more than numbers on a computer screen, entries in a database or figures on a spreadsheet. Perhaps before long we will be known by our biometric data or our DNA code.

Modern Western society has placed us in the middle of an unpleasant paradox. On the one hand, those organisations that watch us know far more about us than we would like them to know.

'They' – as we call them because we don't know who 'they' are – are aware of where we shop and what we shop for, and they know not just our spending habits but our income; they apparently know all about us.

Yet the more these 'somebodies' out there know about us, the less they seem to care. Our problems are dealt with by call centres half a world away; we endure messages from robotic voices trying to convince us that they 'value our custom'; and we receive computer-generated letters overflowing with synthetic friendship: *'Dear Reverend John, we would like to inform you of a wonderful opportunity for you and your family.'* We are known both too well and too little.

In the days ahead I want us to look at Advent, the season of preparation for the coming of Christ. And look at the experience of individuals in the Bible's account.

What we call the Christmas story is full of men and women. Some of them walk onto the pages of Scripture and then – after a brief moment – they walk off. Others that feature more prominently, such as Mary and Joseph, are those you would expect to hear about; others are less well known and some are, perhaps, surprising. But all are relevant. God is love and doesn't just care about the human race *in general* but about people in particular. And that includes you and me.

Prayer: Thank you, Lord, that you know us better than we know ourselves. Thank you that at the beginning of this Advent season, we can know that we are special and valuable in your eyes. Amen.

Ponder: God is love and doesn't just care about the human race in general but about people in particular. That includes me.

THE ANCESTORS: PART 1

This is the genealogy of Jesus the Messiah the son of David, the son of Abraham . . .
(Matthew 1:1)

In this Advent season, the run-up to Christmas, we are looking at the coming of Christ as it affected individuals and how they experienced this extraordinary event.

Let's begin with a group that we can call 'the ancestors of Jesus'.

When it comes to people, Matthew's introduction to Jesus' birth does them in a big way. We get 16 verses of names. Although genealogies don't mean very much to many of us in the West, they do in other parts of the world. For most people, the answer to the question 'Who am I?' includes 'Who do I come from?' Ancestry is part of identity.

Here, this list of names takes us back to Abraham and David – to whom God promised descendants who would be a blessing to the world.

Perhaps the most significant thing about both Abraham and David is that they are people to whom God made promises about descendants. Two thousand years before Christ's birth, God promised Abraham that he would have descendants who would be a blessing to the entire human race. A thousand years later, God promised David that he would have a descendant who would be a far greater king than David would ever be. That king was given the name

Messiah, *'the one who is anointed'*, and the Greek word is the Christ. This list of names is of people through whom God's promises to both Abraham and David are working out. Advent is the culmination of an awesome length of history.

Imagine yourself as a faithful Jew around the time of Jesus' birth: whenever you remembered those age-old promises to Abraham and David you must have felt disappointed that they had not been fulfilled. Yet the reality was that God was about to fulfil those promises; he was just working at his own pace.

In an age of instant everything – credit, coffee, photographs, dating – it is easy to become impatient with God when nothing seems to be happening in our lives. We can assume that the apparent absence of God's action means that he is not active. Yet God works in his own way and to his own timescale. Part of the story of Advent is the revelation that God had been working out his promises to both Abraham and David.

'Is it Christmas yet?' children often ask at this time of year, yet we are often impatient too. God may have promised you something – just be patient!

Prayer: Grant us patience, Lord. As we await your return may we live our lives in the light of eternity. Amen.

Ponder: Is there a situation that doesn't appear to be changing? Allow God to become involved in that situation – circumstances may not change but you will.

THE ANCESTORS: PART 2

This is the genealogy of Jesus the Messiah the son of David, the son of Abraham . . . Judah the father of Perez and Zerah, whose mother was Tamar . . . Salmon the father of Boaz, whose mother was Rahab, Boaz the father of Obed, whose mother was Ruth, Obed the father of Jesse, and Jesse the father of King David. David was the father of Solomon, whose mother had been Uriah's wife, Solomon the father of Rehoboam . . . (Matthew 1:1–7)

In our examination of people involved in the Advent story let us look at the genealogy – that list of who was the father of who – found in the first chapter of Matthew's Gospel, which establishes that Jesus is the long-prophesied descendant of both Abraham and David.

At first glance, we may be struck that this is almost entirely a list of male names. We seem to read only of fathers. Well, that's the way society worked then and Matthew is doing exactly what was expected of him.

Or is he?

There are, in fact, four women mentioned: Tamar, Rahab, Ruth and Solomon's unnamed mother, who was Bathsheba. Even more surprising is that three of them – Tamar, Rahab and Ruth – were non-Jews, and Bathsheba probably was too. Matthew hints that God's purposes are not confined to the Jewish people. The blessing that Jesus the Messiah is going to bring to the world is something that will affect not just the Jewish nation but the whole world.

The other interesting observation is that these women are not 'Good Jewish Mothers' such as Sarah, Rebekah and Rachel. On the contrary, a shadow of guilt hangs over three of the women: Tamar posed as a pagan cult prostitute, Rahab is referred to as a prostitute, and Uriah's wife Bathsheba committed adultery with King David. On the surface, the genealogy gives Jesus an impeccable Jewish background: he is descended from Abraham through David.

The Advent story is focused on people but it is worth noticing that they are very human people – these are people with flaws. In his genealogy, Matthew is making the point that Jesus' human ancestry includes not just the great and the good, but the *'not so great'*, the *'really not very good'* and the *'rather dubious'*.

This is the great principle of grace: God's love is poured out on all – *yes, all* – who will receive it. Jesus is coming to the world not for the good people with a perfect past but for those who are less than good and who have a problem past. There's hope for us all!

Prayer: Thank you, Lord, that your grace is available to everyone who asks. May we at this Advent time rejoice in that fact and endeavour to share this with anyone you bring across our path today. Amen.

Ponder: 'God's love is poured out on all – yes, all – who will receive it.'

ZECHARIAH AND ELIZABETH

In the time of Herod king of Judea there was a priest named Zechariah . . . his wife Elizabeth was also a descendant of Aaron. (Luke 1:5)

If we were writing an account of Jesus' life, we would probably start with who his parents were and then move on to his birth. Luke's Gospel begins by interweaving the accounts of the births of John the Baptist and Jesus. John the Baptist plays a significant part. He is the prologue to the play – he walks on to the stage, gets everyone's attention and then quietly steps into the shadows as Jesus takes centre stage.

At the start of his Gospel, Luke introduces John's parents, a priest called Zechariah and his wife Elizabeth. They are described as being *'righteous in the sight of God, observing all the Lord's commands and decrees blamelessly'* (Luke 1:6). Not many of us would warrant that description! Yet they are childless, a serious matter in a culture where children indicated God's blessing and provided security for old age. We are told that Elizabeth was barren and, as they are both *'well advanced in years'*, they would have presumed that this sad situation was permanent.

Three things are striking here.

The first is that Elizabeth and Zechariah are good people, yet something bad has happened to them. Throughout history people have assumed that, if you are good, God will be so pleased with you that only good things will happen to you. Of course, it doesn't work like that. We all deserve nothing and it is only because of God's grace that we get anything good at all. What is really surprising is not why bad things happen to good people but why good things happen to any of us.

The second thing is that they have been childless for a long time. We are told that they are elderly and therefore must have been praying for a child for years. Imagine how, month by month, their hopes had been dashed.

The final thing is that in the end they are blessed. Indeed, they are blessed more than they can imagine: not just a son, but an *important* son.

Advent is when God breaks into the world with blessing. And he can break into ours, if we will let him.

Prayer: Father God, we give you our disappointments, worries and concerns. Thank you for the reminder that you have broken into this fallen world to bring us hope of a future where there will be no more tears or mourning. In this time of waiting may we live in the knowledge that you have overcome the world. Amen.

Ponder: *'In this world you will have trouble. But take heart! I [Jesus] have overcome the world'* (John 16:33).

ZECHARIAH AND THE ANGEL

An angel of the Lord appeared to him . . . the angel said to him: 'Do not be afraid, Zechariah; your prayer has been heard. Your wife Elizabeth will bear you a son, and you are to call him John.' (Luke 1:11–13)

Advent is about God entering this world in person. In a way that we will never be able to understand, the Maker and Ruler of the universe *humbles himself* in order to become one of Earth's citizens. Given the significance of this, it is not surprising that Jesus' birth is surrounded by supernatural events, particularly the appearance of angels.

This first happens in the centre of the great Temple in Jerusalem. The aged Zechariah is terrified by Gabriel's appearance. He is told that his wife will bear a child, that the infant is to be called John and that he will be a blessing both to his parents and to God's people. The child will bring people back to God and – most importantly – make a people who are prepared for the Lord. It is an awesome promise, but Zechariah queries the angel's pronouncement. *'How can I be sure of this? I am an old man and my wife is well along in years'* (Luke 1:18).

This is not the wisest response, and the angel pronounces God's discipline on unbelief: Zechariah will be silent until John is born.

I think there are two lessons here:

Zechariah goes to serve God but instead God serves him.

With God we always receive more than we give.

Zechariah is 'righteous in the sight of God', yet when it comes to trusting God, he wavers. Zechariah and his wife may have been praying for years for a child. Yet when Zechariah is told by an angel that his prayer is going to be answered, what he in effect says is, 'Now, it's all very well of you to say that but I'm really not convinced.'

Zechariah and Elizabeth have prayed for a child, but over the years he has allowed doubt to wear away the promise. What makes Zechariah's lack of faith worse is that – as every Jew knew – there were precedents for God giving a child to the elderly and childless, most notably to Abraham and Sarah, who were the ancestors of all the Jewish people. Zechariah had forgotten both his own prayers and what God had done in the past. We can often do exactly the same thing.

But God does use very ordinary people, with all their flaws and deficiencies. I find that encouraging and hope you do as well.

Prayer: Lord, we are sorry when we forget what you have done for us in the past. We lift our doubts to you in the safe knowledge that you are trustworthy. Amen.

Ponder: *'I do believe; help me overcome my unbelief!'* (Mark 9:24).

MARY: PART 1

God sent the angel Gabriel to Nazareth, a town in Galilee, to a virgin pledged to be married to a man named Joseph, a descendant of David. The virgin's name was Mary. (Luke 1:26–27)

The angel Gabriel is sent with an extraordinary message to Nazareth, to an unmarried girl called Mary. She will miraculously bear a child who will be the *Son of the Most High*, the promised Messiah who will sit on the throne of David and will rule over Israel for ever in a kingdom that will never end.

Familiarity with the Christmas story makes us overlook the details.

First, in this culture, as in the rural Middle East today – a woman had to belong to someone, and her sexual purity was enormously valued. So at a relatively young age – anything from 12 to 14 – a marriage would be arranged with someone suitable.

There would then follow a legally binding engagement (the *'pledged to be married'* part) in which the girl stayed with her parents under their supervision. Only after this did the formal wedding occur; after which, she moved to her husband's house. These traditions are important in understanding what happens with Mary, who is in the 'in-between stage' of the marriage process: still with her parents but legally bound to Joseph.

What happens is remarkable . . .

Consider the time. At least 400 years have passed since the last book of the Old Testament was written. Silence has fallen on God's people.

Consider the place. Nazareth was as far as you could get from the Temple in Jerusalem and there were longstanding suspicions that here the Jewish faith – and the Jewish people – had become polluted by the non-Jews. *'Galilee of the Gentiles'* is the term used in Isaiah 9. It is not a promising place.

Consider the person. Given Mary's youth, the status of women and that nothing is said about her parents, we may presume that she was, in effect, of no significance. That is reinforced after Jesus is born and she and Joseph give offerings for the infant Jesus: they give the sacrifices expected of poor people.

A nobody girl in a nowhere town, at a time when Jewish history appears to be going nowhere. There is an encouragement here. You may think that you are a nobody, living in a place that might as well be called 'Nowhere' and at a time when nothing much is happening. Well, you know, you may just be in for a heavenly surprise.

Prayer: Lord, may we, like Mary, be open to your leading; may we live for you in the places you have put us. Amen.

Ponder: 'Start by doing what is necessary; then do what is possible; and suddenly you are doing the impossible' (Francis of Assisi).

MARY: PART 2

'I am the Lord's servant,' Mary answered. 'May it be to me according to your word.' Then the angel left her. (Luke 1:38)

The announcement that Gabriel makes to Mary is probably one of the most extraordinary statements ever made to anybody. It's not just that she will have a son from a miraculous conception but that in him all the prophecies of the Old Testament will be fulfilled. The promises she is given are utterly overwhelming and, as she heard them, I wonder if Mary wrestled with three emotions.

Mary must have been afraid. We perceive angels as harmless, but from what we learn in the Bible, angels are holy and powerful, even wise and saintly people are reduced to quivering in fear.

Mary must have been puzzled. The promises are so extensive and extraordinary that even to try and take them in must have been demanding. You can imagine half a dozen questions surfacing in her mind. *Who? What? Why? When?* And of course – *Why me?*

Mary must have faced doubt. What is promised seems to go beyond everything remotely believable. She must have felt that the angel had got the wrong village, the wrong house, the wrong Mary. Indeed, Mary feels obliged to point out to the angel the basic facts of biology: as a virgin she is going to find producing a baby *a little difficult*.

Yet Mary's final response is extraordinary and worthy of praise. *'I am the Lord's servant; may it be to me according to your word.'* There's a contrast here that shouldn't be missed: Zechariah the priest, old in years and full of knowledge, dithers over the angel's words; Mary, a teenager, simply says, *'May it happen as you have said.'*

There are at least two lessons in this:

First, don't let inexperience or youth make you think that God can't use you. Christianity has had two thousand years of the church as a professional organisation, full of educated people, yet, as he did with Mary, God often makes a detour around 'the professionals' and instead uses people who do not meet the *normal criteria.*

Second, when God asks you to do something, just say yes. But, as Mary's example demonstrates, even when fear, puzzlement and doubt are in the air, obedience to God is the best policy. Always was; always will be.

Prayer: Lord, whatever our age may we respond to you as Mary did; help us to be obedient to you in our thoughts, words and deeds. Amen.

Ponder: 'Obedience to God is the best policy. Always was; always will be.'

8th December

ELIZABETH

[Mary] entered Zechariah's home and greeted Elizabeth. When Elizabeth heard Mary's greeting, the baby leaped in her womb, and Elizabeth was filled with the Holy Spirit. In a loud voice she exclaimed: 'Blessed are you among women, and blessed is the child you will bear!' (Luke 1:40–42)

It seems probable that Mary, following Gabriel's announcement that her relative Elizabeth has miraculously become pregnant, heads south as soon as possible to see her.

As a saintly, elderly relative with a priest for a husband Elizabeth is the obvious person to talk things over with. Mary would have been struggling with everything that she had heard. There were not simply the 'theological' issues of who her son was to be but all the implications of being an unmarried mother in a society that had very firm ways of handling teenage girls caught in sexual scandals.

Yet when Mary gets to Elizabeth's house and greets her something happens that changes everything. Elizabeth feels the baby in her womb leaping with joy at the presence of the unborn Jesus. Filled with the Holy Spirit, she declares that the girl before her is *'the mother of my Lord'* and says how blessed Mary is for having believed what God has said.

Notice God's grace to Mary. She must have needed confirmation of what Gabriel had said and here she receives it. She has two things confirmed: she is indeed pregnant and the son she bears is *'Lord'* – the one whom Gabriel has promised would be Son of God, David's heir, the Messiah.

Notice also the characters in this account: an older woman, a teenage girl and two unborn babies. All the more striking is the absence of Zechariah the priest, Elizabeth's husband, the man you might have expected to be the fount of all wisdom.

None of it is as you would expect. It's the Advent principle operating again: *God using unlikely and insignificant people to achieve his purposes.* You could say that in order to achieve his purposes, God avoids the motorways and uses the B-roads instead.

Elizabeth is inspired by the Holy Spirit to call Jesus *'Lord'*. It is the first time this term is used of Jesus but, as Luke will tell us in the Book of Acts, Mary's child will eventually be known by that title across the entire Roman Empire. Advent reminds us that God certainly is in the details. What you do today may seem to be nothing, but if God is involved – a nothing can become everything.

Prayer: Thank you, Lord, that yet again we are reminded that you use each and every one of us to achieve your purposes. May we be willing to hear your promptings today. Amen.

Ponder: 'If God is involved – a nothing can become everything.'

MARY: PART 3

And Mary said: 'My soul glorifies the Lord and my spirit rejoices in God my Saviour.'
(Luke 1:46–47)

In Luke's account of the Advent and the birth of Jesus there is often a note of joy and there are songs. What Mary sings here – known as the *Magnificat* – is one of the most famous.

Three things strike me about the *Magnificat*.

First, Mary celebrates how good God has been to her and makes it clear that she hasn't deserved his goodness. We can only *really* understand what grace is when we are humble enough to realise that we haven't deserved what God has given us.

Second, Mary repeats a theme that we've already heard in Advent: *the promises of the Old Testament are finally coming to fulfilment.* God keeps his promises. That's good to be reminded of.

Third, is a declaration that God will overturn the world's values. Mary declares that God will deal with the proud, the rulers and the rich, and *instead* the humble and the hungry are going to be lifted up. At long last, justice is going to be done.

At this time of year there is so much 'background noise' in the planning, the preparations and the shopping, that it's hard to hear what God wants to say. Mary's deep and thoughtful reflection on what is happening should be a challenge to us to think deeply about what Advent means.

Joy is an emotion that can easily be crowded out of our lives by busyness and worry. We may need to make time to be thoughtful and joyful. It's an extraordinary tragedy that our modern Western Christmas season has become so feverish that the first casualties of the 'festive season' are the joy and peace that are the basis of true festivity.

Finally, if we are tempted to be envious of the rich, powerful and proud because they have everything we think we want, remember the warning of the *Magnificat*.

The God of Advent is the God of reversals: he is the one who brings down the mighty and lifts up the humble.

Feeling high and mighty? – Be careful.

Feeling trampled down? – Be uplifted.

Prayer: Like Mary, may we glorify you and rejoice in you our God and Saviour. For you have done great things for us and you are holy and mighty. You show justice and kindness. May we walk with you all the days of our lives. Amen.

Ponder: 'The God of Advent is the God of reversals: he is the one who brings down the mighty and lifts up the humble.'

JOSEPH: PART 1

Because Joseph her husband was a righteous man and did not want to expose her to public disgrace, he had in mind to divorce her quietly.
(Matthew 1:19)

We know little of Joseph except that he is a carpenter and, as most Jewish young men would have been married by the age of twenty, he is probably in his teens. We don't know how Joseph finds out that Mary is pregnant but when he does he is faced with the appalling certainty that the girl he is legally engaged to is not a virgin and is about to have a child that isn't his.

In this culture, that makes her a shameful woman and her dishonour affects him. The most effective way for Joseph to defend his honour is to accuse her in court in a public divorce. Her conviction would publicly and permanently humiliate Mary but *might* save his reputation. *What is a righteous man to do?*

Eventually, Joseph plans a private divorce, which would avoid any public 'naming and shaming'. It's a brave move, more considerate to Mary and probably far more than the culture expected. However, Joseph would probably still be suspected of being the father.

But God intervenes and an angel appears to Joseph in a dream. God demands an even deeper righteousness: Joseph is told to take Mary home as his wife, that the child is of God and that he is to name him Jesus because *'he will save his people from their sins'* (Matthew 1:21). And – this is the key point – Joseph obeys. Ignoring any allegations that he has betrayed the moral standards of his society, he takes Mary home as his wife, putting her and the child under his protection.

He will deal with any rumours of immorality. He also names the baby Jesus. In doing so, Joseph formally adopts the child into the family of David: he is legally now of the lineage of the kings of Israel.

Defying society's norms, ignoring criticism and taking on something of the inevitable guilt, Joseph obeys God, taking Mary and the unborn child to be his own.

We need to seek this sort of righteousness and we must be prepared to ignore the critical voices of those about us.

We need to look to God for what he calls us to do.

Sometimes, especially when, like Joseph, we stand up for the weak and the defenceless, such righteousness may be costly.

Prayer: May we, like Joseph, be righteous in our lives. Give us compassion for those facing difficult and complicated circumstances. May we have your wisdom to see circumstances as you see them. Amen.

Ponder: *'Instruct the wise, and they will be wiser still. Teach the righteous and they will add to their learning'* (Proverbs 9:9).

ELIZABETH AND ZECHARIAH

When it was time for Elizabeth to have her baby, she gave birth to a son . . . Everyone who heard this wondered about it, asking, 'What then is this child going to be?' For the Lord's hand was with him. (Luke 1:57,66)

There is great joy as Elizabeth gives birth to a son. Zechariah, however, remains dumb as a result of the angel Gabriel's rebuke. Then, at the important event of circumcision, something happens. The family has decided the baby is going to be called Zechariah after his father but Elizabeth defies them, announcing that his name will be John.

The mute Zechariah confirms in writing that John is indeed the name the child is to be given. As he does this he is able to speak once again. What does he say? Well, Luke tells us that he starts to praise God. John's birth and the events surrounding it become the talk of the region with everybody asking, 'What is this child going to be?' *What does this mean?*

Let me make two observations.

Looking at the Advent accounts, you can't help but feel that the priest Zechariah draws the short straw. A few thoughtless words to the angel Gabriel and he is struck dumb for nine months. It's a good illustration of the principle that power and privilege brings responsibility and that as a priest he really should have known better. Nevertheless, we find here that he has used his enforced silence to good use. When he can speak he praises God.

There's an uncomfortable lesson for us here. Sometimes, for our own long-term good, God does discipline us, but it's a good reminder that when faced with God's blessings, praise not protest should be a priority.

The second observation is that these events surrounding the birth of John make everybody think, 'What is this child going to be?' John the Baptist is going to be the one who issues the great wake-up call to the sleeping nation of Israel and he starts in that role from his very birth.

He raises questions, issues warnings and challenges everyone. That question of the people – 'What is this child going to be?' – is a very appropriate one for us during Advent. This can be a time of extraordinary superficiality, where we simply note the facts and move on swiftly.

We observe that Advent is about the infant Jesus and we stop there. We need to go beyond simply noting facts to considering significance. We need to be those who ask that much deeper question: 'What is this child going to be?' In the case of Jesus the answer is someone far greater and far more wonderful than we can ever imagine.

Prayer: Dear Lord, prompt us to remember that the trimmings of Christmas are inconsequential compared to the gift of Jesus Christ. May we rejoice that your birth changed the course of history and marvel that you still transform lives today. Amen.

Ponder: *'For to us a child is born, to us a son is given, and the government will be on his shoulders. And he will be called Wonderful Counsellor, Mighty God, Everlasting Father, Prince of Peace'* (Isaiah 9:6).

ZECHARIAH

His father Zechariah was filled with the Holy Spirit and prophesied: 'Praise be to the Lord, the God of Israel, because he has come to his people and redeemed them.' (Luke 1:67–68)

This is recorded as one of Luke's songs, sometimes called the *Benedictus*. It's rich in Old Testament references and it's all about a problem and a solution.

Zechariah recognises a problem. There's a lot in this song about enemies, darkness and the shadow of death. It may sound as if Zechariah has a gloomy view but he lived in difficult times. God's people Israel were crushed under the brutal political domination and they suffered under a decaying religious system of their own that was in need of renewal. The people were weighed down and oppressed and they needed divine intervention. Actually, that's the reality for a lot of people today.

Zechariah doesn't get bogged down by the problem but focuses on the solution: a person, a deliverer, described as a mighty Saviour from the royal line of his servant David, a 'rescuer' and 'the Lord'. Zechariah is sure that this great figure is going to bring salvation through forgiveness of sins, light to those who sit in darkness and guidance into the path of peace. Zechariah sees God's deliverance as being so guaranteed that he talks about it in the past tense: God has visited and has redeemed his people, he has sent us a mighty Saviour, we have been rescued from our enemies. Zechariah is so confident that the God who has promised these things will deliver them that he effectively considers them a 'done deal'.

There is a lot to think about in Zechariah's prophetic song. Perhaps you can readily identify with the problem: the need for deliverance. Perhaps your life is in darkness. You may even know something about enemies or about being hated. Well, if you know something of the problem, take hold of the solution: the Lord about to come in Jesus.

An easily overlooked feature of Zechariah's song is that his long-awaited son, John, gets only a brief mention. Zechariah sees John's importance simply in the way that he prepares the way for Jesus. This humility is exactly the attitude that John the Baptist shows, decades later. Then, John says of himself and Jesus: *'He must become greater; I must become less'* (John 3:30).

The very best that any of us can do is what John did: prepare the way for the Lord.

Prayer: Lord, as we remember Zechariah's prophecy may we praise you that you are our Deliverer. However we feel at this moment, may we truly embrace the hope that you give to us, which enables us to go out and prepare the way for you to work in our world today. Amen.

Ponder: *'Jesus looked at them and said, "With man this is impossible, but with God all things are possible"'* (Matthew 19:26).

CAESAR AUGUSTUS

In those days Caesar Augustus issued a decree that a census should be taken of the entire Roman world . . . And everyone went to their own town to register. So Joseph also went up from the town of Nazareth in Galilee to Judea, to Bethlehem. (Luke 2:1,3–4)

Prophecies have been given, John has been born, Jesus has been conceived miraculously and Joseph has agreed to adopt the child into the kingly line of David. All is ready. Well, almost.

There is just one issue: Joseph and Mary are in totally the wrong place. The Old Testament prophecies say that David's heir must be born in Bethlehem. So for this prophecy to be fulfilled, Mary and Joseph must somehow leave Nazareth and end up in Bethlehem. Luke tells us that they ended up in the right place because, far away in Rome, the emperor had decided to count heads and had put a senior bureaucrat, Publius Quirinius, in charge. The result is that Joseph has to travel southwards, taking his pregnant wife with him.

There are several things here.

First, a reminder that in the Advent story we deal with history. It is rooted in the world of Emperor Augustus and Governor Quirinius and, if it is true history, then it is significant.

Second, we see God nudging the most important person in the known world so that he sets in motion a complex international bureaucratic procedure resulting in a peasant girl giving birth in just the right place. Here, God uses the mighty to serve his purposes.

Third, where the focus in the Advent accounts has been small-scale and local, now Rome, the emperor and the Empire's administration make an appearance. This is no coincidence: the Gospel writers tell us that what is about to happen in Bethlehem will have a vast significance for the emperor and the Empire. Luke is hinting that this is going to be part of a global story.

Finally, there is comfort here. There are still many empire-like organisations and companies in this world. It is easy to feel vulnerable and helpless before such powers yet this census reminds us that standing above these earthly powers is the heavenly power of God. Caesars, and those like them, may think they control the world, but the reality is otherwise.

If we know Christ then the one who rules the nations is on our side.

Prayer: When we look at the world's problems today they seem overwhelming, Lord. Teach us to trust you in all circumstances and to see your solutions to problems. Help us to know what to be involved in so that we can play our part in being your hands and feet in this world. Amen.

Ponder: 'We ourselves feel that what we are doing is nothing more than a drop in the ocean. But the ocean would be less because of that missing drop' (Mother Teresa).

JESUS

The time came for the baby to be born, and [Mary] gave birth to her firstborn, a son. She wrapped him in cloths and placed him in a manger, because there was no guest room available for them. (Luke 2:6–7)

I wonder if you spotted something different in this reading? Instead of 'no room . . . in the inn' we had *'no guest room'*. It's a recognition that the Greek word traditionally translated 'inn' is better translated as 'guest room'. It makes more sense because given that Joseph was of the line of David he could probably have knocked on almost any door, listed his ancestry, been identified as a distant relative and been offered a room.

What seems likely is that the house where Joseph and Mary planned to stay had only two rooms: one for the family and one for the guests.

For some reason – possibly the census – the guest room was full. The only alternative was the lower part of the house, where the animals were usually kept. Of all the traditions associated with Jesus' birth, one of the most reliable is that he was born in a cave, and it's quite likely that the lower part of the house would have been cut in a cave-like way from the rock.

So, the baby is born, wrapped in strips of cloth and placed in the manger – the animal feed trough. That this was highly

unusual is suggested by the shepherds being told that 'the baby in a manger' is a sign.

With Jesus' birth we come to something quite extraordinarily profound. Christian teaching is that, in this baby, God was somehow entering his own creation. The all-powerful Maker and Sustainer of everything – from tiniest bacteria to largest galaxy – is reduced to a few pounds of helpless flesh.

This is the extraordinary truth that we call the incarnation – that, in Jesus, God became one of us. It is an extraordinary descent from highest majesty to lowest insignificance, from unbelievable wealth to desperate poverty. What can we learn from this? Well, we get some idea of exactly how much God loves us; being born in this context set the pattern for the rest of Jesus' earthly life.

There is another thing worth noticing – the phrase that Luke uses: *'She wrapped him in cloths and placed him in a manger . . .'* At the end of Luke's Gospel, in chapter 23, we read that Joseph of Arimathea went to Pilate and asked for Jesus' body and *'then he took [the body] down, wrapped it in linen cloth and placed it in a tomb cut in the rock'.* The parallel is very striking.

For our sake Jesus became the lowest of the low, quite literally from the cradle to the cross.

Prayer: Lord, as we at this Advent time marvel at the fact you became human in order to show your great love for us, thank you that by your death and resurrection we can now know freedom from the past, new life today and a hope for the future. Amen.

Ponder: 'For our sake Jesus became the lowest of the low, quite literally from the cradle to the cross.'

THE MIDWIFE

[Mary] gave birth to her firstborn, a son.

(Luke 2:7)

Let's consider the midwife.

'Hold on,' I hear you say, 'there is no midwife.' I agree: there is no Gospel account of a midwife. But there must surely have been one – it is unlikely that Mary managed to deliver her firstborn without another woman alongside her. Probably from the extended family, some distantly connected aunt or cousin of Joseph's, who would have been there to assist.

What a responsibility! Delivering the Son of God into the world! Not that the midwife would have realised who it was. Yet despite the importance of her task there is no record of her at all.

But thirty years later, in her old age, did she perhaps recognise in the description of Jesus of Nazareth, born in Bethlehem, the child she had delivered? I believe we can learn about two important things from the midwife and her omission from history: fame and significance.

Because we now live in a celebrity culture we tend to feel that our best actions deserve publicity; we think of fame as being the reward for doing good things. Yet it doesn't always work like that. In the world not everybody gets paid in the currency of fame.

We all know those who do good works and get no reward: no medals, no invitations to the Palace, no letters after their name. Just silence. For Christians, fame should be incidental. All that matters is doing what God wants.

It may well be that what you're involved in is important but you know that it's unappreciated. You have done, or are doing, something vital – a job, child rearing, a carer – and you do it well but everybody takes you for granted. Well, it's happened to other people and the great consolation is that God knows what you do.

The midwife of Bethlehem also suggests something about significance. Two of life's great questions focus on the meaning of our existence. There is the cry of youth: 'What am I going to do with my life?' and there is the cry of old age: 'What did I do with my life?' We all want to look forward or backward for significance.

I think the case of our midwife helps us here. She may very soon have forgotten this particular delivery, yet these few hours were of supreme importance. She was there at the right place at the right time with the right skills. Our lives may work in the same way; unknown to us, we may have been of enormous significance.

We can be anonymous to the world but no one is anonymous to God.

Prayer: As we go about our day, may we remember that you know what we do. However insignificant we may feel, may we remember that in you we have significance. Amen.

Ponder: *'Serve wholeheartedly, as if you were serving the Lord, not people'* (Ephesians 6:7).

THE SHEPHERDS: PART 1

And there were shepherds living out in the fields nearby, keeping watch over their flocks at night. (Luke 2:8)

After centuries of expectation, the long-promised Messiah is born – and high in the night skies an angel appears and 'the glory of the Lord' shines out. It must have been awesomely, dazzlingly impressive. Then something occurs that is without precedent in Scripture: 'the heavenly host' appears – an entire army of angels. It is God's way of making the point that, for all the obscurity and apparent insignificance of the baby in the stable, what has happened is extraordinarily significant.

Shepherds were pretty close to the bottom of the Jewish social pyramid. Yet it is to them that the angel speaks. The heavens reveal their dazzling glory not to the High Priest, not to Herod, not to Quirinius, but to shepherds, whose job meant that they rarely made it to the synagogue. These were working men at work, *'keeping watch over their flocks'*.

'You will find a baby wrapped in cloths and lying in a manger.' It is a sign not of glory but of poverty, a sign of the sort of Messiah this is. The obvious place for angels to appear is five miles away, in the magnificent Jerusalem Temple, the very centre of the world for Jews. There, in the holy of holies, was the divinely approved meeting place between man and God. Yet on this night the glory of God appears out in a farmer's fields.

JESUS

The time came for the baby to be born, and [Mary] gave birth to her firstborn, a son. She wrapped him in cloths and placed him in a manger, because there was no guest room available for them. (Luke 2:6–7)

I wonder if you spotted something different in this reading? Instead of 'no room . . . in the inn' we had *'no guest room'*. It's a recognition that the Greek word traditionally translated 'inn' is better translated as 'guest room'. It makes more sense because given that Joseph was of the line of David he could probably have knocked on almost any door, listed his ancestry, been identified as a distant relative and been offered a room.

What seems likely is that the house where Joseph and Mary planned to stay had only two rooms: one for the family and one for the guests.

For some reason – possibly the census – the guest room was full. The only alternative was the lower part of the house, where the animals were usually kept. Of all the traditions associated with Jesus' birth, one of the most reliable is that he was born in a cave, and it's quite likely that the lower part of the house would have been cut in a cave-like way from the rock.

So, the baby is born, wrapped in strips of cloth and placed in the manger – the animal feed trough. That this was highly

Second, we see God nudging the most important person in the known world so that he sets in motion a complex international bureaucratic procedure resulting in a peasant girl giving birth in just the right place. Here, God uses the mighty to serve his purposes.

Third, where the focus in the Advent accounts has been small-scale and local, now Rome, the emperor and the Empire's administration make an appearance. This is no coincidence: the Gospel writers tell us that what is about to happen in Bethlehem will have a vast significance for the emperor and the Empire. Luke is hinting that this is going to be part of a global story.

Finally, there is comfort here. There are still many empire-like organisations and companies in this world. It is easy to feel vulnerable and helpless before such powers yet this census reminds us that standing above these earthly powers is the heavenly power of God. Caesars, and those like them, may think they control the world, but the reality is otherwise.

If we know Christ then the one who rules the nations is on our side.

Prayer: When we look at the world's problems today they seem overwhelming, Lord. Teach us to trust you in all circumstances and to see your solutions to problems. Help us to know what to be involved in so that we can play our part in being your hands and feet in this world. Amen.

Ponder: 'We ourselves feel that what we are doing is nothing more than a drop in the ocean. But the ocean would be less because of that missing drop' (Mother Teresa).

God is again lifting up the humble.

The Gospels of both Matthew and Luke point out that outcasts and outsiders were involved. Matthew highlights the religious outsiders – the Gentiles – who honour Jesus and are honoured by God; Luke highlights the social outsiders – the poor and downtrodden. Those who were previously excluded from salvation can now rejoice; social outcasts are included.

Perhaps the most important thing is the location of this extraordinary vision of heaven: because of this child, access to God is no longer going to be focused on one magnificent building in Jerusalem. From the death of Jesus onwards the world will have access to God, not through sacrifices in the Temple in Jerusalem but through Jesus.

Above Bethlehem the sky rips open and the heavenly host is seen; it's a hint that one day the whole earth will be open to God's glory.

Because of this baby, wherever we are, we now have access to God and his salvation, deliverances and healing.

Prayer: Lord, we praise you that because of Jesus we have access to you and your saving, healing power. Help us to not take this for granted but to live our lives in the freedom that Jesus has purchased for us. Amen.

Ponder: Because of Jesus, wherever we are, we now have access to God and his salvation, deliverance and healing.

THE SHEPHERDS: PART 2

The shepherds returned, glorifying and praising God for all the things they had heard and seen, which were just as they had been told.
(Luke 2:20)

In what happens to the shepherds we can see five stages of faith:

- **First, revelation**. *'An angel of the Lord appeared to them, and the glory of the Lord shone around them, and they were terrified'* (Luke 2:9).

  The shepherds become instantly aware of the glory and majesty of God; they realise how great and holy he is and how little and dirty they are – and they are afraid.

- **Second, proclamation**. *'Do not be afraid. I bring you good news of great joy'* (Luke 2:10).

  This is not just news, it is good news about a child who is the Saviour, the one who will free men and women from all their sins. In Jesus we meet our Saviour and Deliverer. It's no wonder that the shepherds' fear is replaced by joy.

- **Third, reaction**. *'So they hurried off and found Mary and Joseph, and the baby, who was lying in the manger'* (Luke 2:16).

God breaks into the shepherds' lives and they hear the good news and do something about it.

- **Fourth, affirmation**. The shepherds tell everybody the truth of what they have seen.

- **Fifth, adoration**. The shepherds praised and worshipped God. Fear had completely turned around into joy. The glory poured down from heaven was now being directed back up to God.

The shepherds are a good model for followers of Jesus both then and now.

Have we given a reaction to what we have heard? We may have been touched by Jesus, but have we responded by going to him and worshipping him?

Do we know anything of affirmation? Have we, like the shepherds, affirmed the truth that Jesus is God's Deliverer? Have we witnessed to who Jesus is?

Finally, in our lives do we show adoration? Do we glorify and praise God for all we have seen and heard? Let us tune into the melody of heaven.

Prayer: Lord, may we be aware of your revelation, may we see your creation as you have intended, may we be attentive to your intervening in our world and may we acknowledge you as our Saviour and Lord. May we, like the shepherds, tune into the melody of heaven. Amen.

Ponder: *'For God so loved the world that he gave his one and only Son, that whoever believes in him shall not perish but have eternal life'* (John 3:16).

MARY: PART 4

But Mary treasured up all these things and pondered them in her heart. (Luke 2:19)

The Christmas story is action-packed; it's a story of good and evil: there's an innocent young girl, her husband and baby, a bad king, angels and real drama – angels appear and kings walk in with oriental splendour.

Actually, for most of us that sense of non-stop action fits with our experience of the Advent season. We are in perpetual motion.

Yet here in the middle of this continuous, action-filled account – in the eye of the storm – there is . . . silence. We read that Mary *'treasured up all these things and pondered them in her heart'.*

To treasure things means to value them. Rather like those favourite photos we display so that we are always reminded of them. Mary did this with what happened; she thought about everything, not just once but repeatedly. The Greek word for pondered means 'tying or bringing everything together'. She tried to bring the threads together, to make sense of what was happening. She meditated on what had happened.

Her song – the *Magnificat* – shows that she was immersed in God's word. She had not simply memorised Scripture, but had thought it through. Yes, Jesus was the son of God, but he was also the son of Mary and here his mother sets a good example. Mary is not just the mother of Jesus, she is the model of faith.

In recent decades we have lost the art of pondering. We have exchanged depth of knowledge for breadth of experience and it may not have been a good exchange. The truths of Christianity are not simply facts – we must not only possess truth but have to let it possess us.

It is all too easy to let the Christmas season surge over us like some great wave of events and for us to emerge from the other end weary but unchanged. We need to be more like Mary and to think through all that it means.

A Charles Wesley hymn includes the following lines:

> 'Our God contracted to a span
> Incomprehensibly made Man.'

That's what Christmas is about: God somehow became baby-sized.

This year, make some time, make some space and make some quiet. And then, as far as you can, ponder the truth that, in this baby, God himself was coming into the world to rescue and redeem you.

Prayer: Father God, as we go through the countdown to Christmas, may we be aware of who you are and what you have done for us. Help us, like Mary, to ponder so that our relationship with you can deepen and our knowledge of you be expanded. Amen.

Ponder: As we light candles this Christmas time, pause to thank Jesus that he came into this world to be a light for us.

THE MAGI: PART 1

Magi from the east came to Jerusalem and asked, 'Where is the one who has been born king of the Jews? We saw his star when it rose and have come to worship him.' (Matthew 2:1–2)

We now come to the three wise men. The Bible calls them Magi – the best translation is probably 'astrologers'. They were people who studied the stars looking for the meaning of events and hints about the future.

In ancient times astrologers often believed that God had allowed the heavens to reveal something of the future. This makes a certain amount of sense: the movement of the moon controlled the tides; the stars' motion measured out the seasons; and the sun brought life. In an uncertain world, any warning of what unpleasantness might be around the corner was eagerly sought.

The steady, unstoppable and majestic movement of stars and planets suggested that if God wasn't going to tell you what was going to happen, his large-scale handiwork might. It's not unreasonable to think of the ancient astrologers as the forerunners of government scientific advisers and they were probably the brightest and best of their society. Maybe that translation 'wise men' is actually the best one.

We don't really know what it was that the astrologers saw in the heavens but, whatever it was, it was significant enough for them to collect gifts and head off across Arabia on camels. A king was going to be born in Judaea – a king so significant that the very heavens proclaimed his coming. This was something they were not going to miss.

There is no indication that Matthew or Luke knew of each other's accounts of Jesus' birth, and there are some striking and delightful contrasts. In Luke we get the shepherds: local, rural, home-grown Jewish boys – not well educated. In Matthew we get the Magi: wealthy, exotically foreign, sophisticated, non-Jewish and highly educated.

The child born in Bethlehem is for everyone.

It doesn't matter today whether you are rich or poor, sophisticated or rustic, educated or illiterate, Jewish or non-Jewish, religious or non-religious. Nothing has changed in two thousand years. The good news of Jesus is for absolutely everybody.

You may have three degrees or have left school at 16; you may have a fortune in the bank or be staring at a pile of final demands. You may identify with shepherds or see yourself as one of the Magi. Whoever you are, wherever you are, Jesus wants you to come to him.

Prayer: Thank you for the reminder that Jesus came into this world for every single one of us. May we be ready to share this truth with our families, friends, neighbours and colleagues through our actions, attitudes and words. Amen.

Ponder: 'Whoever you are, wherever you are, Jesus wants you to come to him.'

HEROD THE GREAT

Herod called the Magi secretly and found out from them the exact time the star had appeared. He sent them to Bethlehem and said, 'Go and make a careful search for the child. As soon as you find him, report to me, so that I too may go and worship him.' (Matthew 2:7–8)

Some people feel that King Herod is too nasty to belong in the Christmas story. Known as 'Herod the Great' his achievements were legendary. He had outlasted countless rebellions and outmanoeuvred innumerable coups. Only half Jewish by birth and not terribly committed to the Jewish religion, Herod always felt vulnerable.

Jesus' birth probably occurred towards the end of Herod's life. By this point, the aged Herod was politically and mentally unstable; his remarkable instinct for survival had degenerated into a deep, ruthless and furious paranoia. And so, into Herod's city of Jerusalem, the Magi came – and their arrival would have been impossible to overlook.

Yet for all their wisdom, these men asked precisely the wrong question. People like Herod inevitably have a network of informers and it is presumably through them that he heard what they were asking. He consults his religious advisers and then summons the Magi to a secret meeting. Herod has lost none of his cunning and when someone with his track record detects a threat it's time for everybody to be very concerned.

If we remove evil from the Christmas story, we create an unreal world and water down the significance of the message of Christmas, that, in this infant, God himself has come to do battle with the powers of evil.

Ironically, the idea that this Messiah has come to fight evil is a truth that Herod seems to have sensed, that the coming of the Messiah was such bad news for him that it could only be dealt with by brutal force. He knows that this child is a threat to him and to all like him. This has not changed.

To all who love him and all he stands for, Jesus offers the promise of an indestructible hope; yet to all who have contempt for him, his coming brings inescapable judgement. The birth of the child in Bethlehem proclaims to the whole world, 'God's justice is coming.'

That's a challenge that the world needs to hear.

Prayer: Lord, as we anticipate you coming again the knowledge of your perfect justice is a source of rejoicing. You see this world as it is with all its inequality, corruption and darkness. We know that in the end you will triumph. Help us to be your hands and feet to bring this hope to many struggling today. Amen.

Ponder: *'But do not forget this one thing, dear friends: with the Lord a day is like a thousand years, and a thousand years are like a day. The Lord is not slow in keeping his promise, as some understand slowness. Instead he is patient with you, not wanting anyone to perish, but everyone to come to repentance'* (2 Peter 3:8–9).

THE CLERGY

When [Herod] had called together all the people's chief priests and teachers of the law, he asked them where the Messiah was to be born. (Matthew 2:4)

We are looking at the experiences of various people during the events of the first Christmas and this is the one that troubles me the most: it involves the 'seriously religious' people. These people do not come out well in the Christmas story.

These are the good guys; they are the keepers of the law, the teachers. These are God's people up against an evil king. And sadly they don't even put up a fight.

There is a prayer of confession in the *Book of Common Prayer*, which says, 'We have left undone those things which we ought to have done, and we have done those things which we ought not to have done, and there is no health in us.' It acknowledges that there are both sins of omission – failing to do what is right – and sins of commission – doing what is wrong. Both are present here.

The sin that the religious authorities commit is to tell Herod where the Messiah is to be born. They must have known that, when faced with a threat, Herod shifted into 'psycho' mode and the blood flowed. Yet in Luke's description of their meeting we see no hint of the religious authorities having any desire to protect their potential Messiah: no hiding of the key text.

Instead, they simply respond to the king's request with a submissive, 'It's Bethlehem in Judea, your Majesty.' To make matters worse they then quote Micah 5:2 with its statement that the child born there will not simply be Messiah, but ruler over Israel. Anything more inclined to trigger an outbreak of pre-emptive murderous rage is hard to imagine.

The good that the religious authorities omit is to find the Messiah and worship him themselves. There is no mention in the Gospels that the religious world bothered to take the five-mile trip south to Bethlehem.

It isn't very impressive, is it? Given that so many of us approaching this Christmas season fit firmly in the category of 'religious people' we really need to ask what went wrong here. I suggest it comes down to fear.

The religious authorities probably supplied the right answer to Herod because they feared for their lives. Yet this sort of cowardice is actually idolatry and in the Old Testament it is condemned. We live in a culture where it has become 'popular' to be anti-Christian, so it's very tempting to keep quiet about Christ at Christmas.

Let's not be afraid of fear. Let us stand up for our faith.

Prayer: Give us a boldness and a love, Lord, to share the true meaning of Christmas with those around us. Amen.

Ponder: 'While many things seem impossible from a human standpoint, in the realm of prayer there are no impossibilities' (Brother Andrew).

THE MAGI: PART 2

On coming to the house, they saw the child with his mother Mary, and they bowed down and worshipped him. Then they opened their treasures and presented him with gifts of gold, frankincense and myrrh. (Matthew 2:11)

The star that led the Magi reappears over Bethlehem and they follow it and find the house. Bethlehem was a quiet, agricultural and respectably Jewish village. Imagine the entourage of the Magi arriving: two worlds are colliding.

The Magi enter and see Mary and the child. They bow down and worship him and offer him gifts: gold, frankincense and myrrh. What's going on here? God's good news is being revealed to those who are not of the Jewish faith. Matthew is hinting at something that will become clear with Jesus' final words: *'Go and make disciples of all nations . . .'* In cinema terms the visit of the Magi is like a trailer for a forthcoming feature – the new, global world of the church.

The Magi are also models for faith.

- **They searched for Jesus.** The Magi's journey to faith – perhaps their journey of faith – was not easy. If they came from Babylon, their journey would have taken them forty days. If you are searching for Jesus, take encouragement from this; your road may be long but if you persist you will find him.

- **They were overjoyed at encountering Jesus.** We read that when they saw the star they were overjoyed.

  And for all the problems that may come with turning to Christ, this pattern remains. To find Jesus is to find joy.

- **They worshipped Jesus.** As the Magi kneeled before the infant we have no idea what was going through their minds. They knew very little about who he was, but they bowed down and worshipped him.

- **They offered Jesus gifts.** Putting aside any symbolic interpretation of the gifts we can simply see this action as them giving him what was costly to them. We cannot offer Jesus cheap discipleship.

We must give him what he is worth. Not just in treasure, but also with our time and talents. In 1872 Christina Rossetti wrote 'In the Bleak Midwinter'. The last verse reads:

'What can I give Him, poor as I am?
If I were a shepherd, I would bring a lamb;
If I were a Wise Man, I would do my part;
Yet what I can I give Him: give my heart.'

The Magi are models for us: to search for Jesus, to experience joy, to worship and to offer him what we have and are to him.

Prayer: Like the Wise Men, may we search for you, may we know your joy that gives us strength and may we worship you with all our heart and soul. Amen.

Ponder: *'Ask and it will be given to you; seek and you will find; knock and the door will be opened to you'* (Matthew 7:7).

JOSEPH: PART 2

An angel of the Lord appeared to Joseph in a dream. 'Get up,' he said, 'take the child and his mother and escape to Egypt. Stay there until I tell you, for Herod is going to search for the child to kill him.' (Matthew 2:13)

Consider the events in which Joseph plays a particular part:

- Mary becomes pregnant by the Holy Spirit and Joseph chooses to divorce her – but an angel intervenes.

- Joseph is forced by the decree of Caesar Augustus to go to Bethlehem.

- To fulfil religious law, Joseph takes the child to the Temple and meets Simeon and Anna.

- Joseph is warned by an angel to take Mary and the child to Egypt.

There are two sorts of people in life: those who make events happen and those who can only react to events. Joseph is in the second group. Things happen to him and he has to respond: his fiancée becomes supernaturally pregnant; his plans for a quiet divorce are quashed by angelic intervention; he is summoned to Bethlehem by an imperial bureaucracy; and he ends up having to take the family into Egypt as refugees.

We can learn from Joseph; there are three commendable things about him.

First, Joseph is righteous. He is introduced to us as a righteous man and in everything he does 'being righteous' seems to be a central feature. He comes over as the sort of man whose only concern is to do what is right.

Second, Joseph is responsive. Twice an angel appears to him in a dream and gives him instructions and that is enough for him to act on. Some people complain that God never speaks to them. My theory is that God rarely bothers speaking to people who are not going to obey him. Joseph quite simply does what he is told.

Third, Joseph is reliable. Yes, things happen to Joseph that he might not have chosen. He gets orders from angels in dreams and he follows them reliably. Mary gets to Bethlehem, they end up with shelter and eventually the family makes it safely to Egypt. He is 'a safe pair of hands' – and, given the value of what he is cradling in his hands when he holds the baby Jesus, that is a pretty important quality.

Faced with an extraordinary task Joseph simply plays his part well. He is righteous, responsive and reliable.

We might prefer other attributes but to be known by these is high praise indeed.

Prayer: Lord, as we consider Joseph help us to live a righteous life. May we be ready to follow instructions and obey your commands. May we be known as reliable people in all areas of our life. Amen.

Ponder: Righteous, responsive and reliable – with the Holy Spirit at work in our lives we can have these attributes.

SIMEON AND ANNA

Simeon took him in his arms and praised God . . . [Anna] gave thanks to God and spoke about the child to all who were looking forward to the redemption of Jerusalem. (Luke 2:28,38)

By Boxing Day, preachers want to put Christmas behind them and start to think about the New Year. So the story of Simeon and Anna – and 'the Presentation at the Temple' – is often overlooked.

Joseph and Mary treat the new baby according to the Jewish traditions of their day: the baby was circumcised and then, forty days after the birth, Mary and Joseph take the child to the Temple in Jerusalem for Mary's ritual purification and Jesus' dedication to God as the firstborn son.

At the Temple they meet two people.

The first is Simeon. He has been told by the Holy Spirit that he will not die without seeing the Messiah and he has been summoned to the Temple on this day. Simeon takes the infant Jesus, praises God because of him and prophetically declares that he has now seen salvation and that the child will be a blessing to Jew and Gentile. But the baby will be a mixed blessing for the people of Israel, causing some to rise and some to fall, and Mary will know bitter pain because of his ministry.

The second encounter is with Anna, an aged prophetess who recognises in the baby the fulfilment of God's promises to Israel. There is much here to encourage and challenge us. Notice, first, how 'religious duty' is not incompatible with the working of the Holy Spirit. Mary, Joseph and Jesus are in the Temple to fulfil the Old Testament Law. Yet God works in that ritual duty through his Holy Spirit. It is a reminder to us that churchgoing and doing those things that we consider to be our duty do not exclude us from works of the Holy Spirit.

Notice, too, that God uses the elderly. Our culture has little time for senior citizens and old age often comes with a loss of hope. Not so with Simeon and Anna: they have hope. Time waiting for God is never time wasted.

Simeon highlights Jesus' significance, declaring, *'For my eyes have seen your salvation'* (Luke 2:30). The infant is not going to talk about how people are to be saved but will be the means through which they are saved. Simeon also says that the child is to be *'a light for revelation to the Gentiles, and the glory of your people Israel'* (Luke 2:32), that is, the good news will go out across the world, to all people.

Salvation, light to the world, the glory of Israel – will all be accomplished not through the Temple building but through this child. In a world where we can often feel reduced to insignificance, we need to remember the baby in the Temple. Sometimes the little things are vastly more significant than the big ones.

Prayer: The example of Simeon and Anna's faithfulness is inspiring; may we see you as they saw you – a light to reveal God to the nations. Amen.

Ponder: It doesn't matter what age you are, God can use you if you allow him to.

YOU?

God sent his Son, born of a woman, born under the law, to redeem those under the law, that we might receive adoption to sonship.
(Galatians 4:4–5)

We have followed the Advent story. We have looked at the Advent principle that God chooses to work through the little people, the marginalised and the outcasts. We have also seen that, in Jesus, God's grace extends beyond one nation to the whole world.

There are facts and there are experiences and the events of the Nativity should not be reduced to bare facts; the reality is that they must be experienced. The Advent story, the great story of God coming into our world as a human being, demands a response.

The Advent story is not just a story but a drama and if you have ever been to a musical or a play you will know what happens after the final curtain. While the audience applaud, the cast comes onto the stage and takes a bow.

As we conclude these Advent meditations, imagine something similar. The curtain has just fallen on the drama and, as you applaud, the curtain rises again, revealing people and scenery.

At the front is a semicircle of people. Centre stage, with the spotlight shining on him, is the infant Jesus. Immediately behind him are Mary and Joseph, who gaze on the infant;

perhaps we should add the anonymous midwife next to them? On one side are the shepherds, staring at the Christ-child with wonderment. On the other side are the shepherds and the Magi worshipping. On the edge, we can also make out the figures of Simeon and Anna.

We now notice that further back and barely visible in the darkness of the stage are, to one side, the empty thrones of Herod and Caesar and the deserted counting table of Quirinius. On the other side, also in the shadows and equally deserted, is the Temple. Caesar, Herod, the governor, the priests and religious lawyers have gone.

Now, as the audience continues to applaud, something strange happens. The cast on stage beckons us to join them.

The invitation is clear. Come and join the worship of the child! See, in this infant, all that you need: salvation, forgiveness and hope.

The question is for you, and you alone, to answer.

Do you step forward and add your worship to theirs? Does the Nativity story include you? This story – more than any other story – demands from us not simply hearing, or even appreciation. It demands our belief and involvement.

Prayer: 'O holy Child of Bethlehem descend to us, we pray. Cast out our sin and enter in, be born in us today. We hear the Christmas angels, the great glad tidings tell, O come to us, abide with us, our Lord Immanuel' ('O Little Town of Bethlehem', Phillips Brooks).